CW00735326

Sincerely Insincere
Written by Aaron Schulman

Dedicated to my girls:
Chandler, Shiloh & Robin

I gave you walls, I gave you food, I gave you a roof over your head,
I gave you clothes. I gave you toys for your birthdays and holidays and
random Wednesdays walking through Walmart and you wanted
something.

I gave you life and hopefully fond memories to look back on.
I gave you a world that I built from scratch that I worked hard to get.
I gave you all the love I have, I gave you everything I could muster and
more than I ever knew I ever had. I gave my life to you, I never regret a
single second of it and I would do it a million times again and more.

And yet somehow....
Even after all of that...
You still gave me more.
So much more.
Thank you.

Love, Dad.

# Table of Contents

## 1. Today Again

Oh, what a day today has been
Until tomorrow's today again

For when tomorrow becomes today
And today is now the past
The day after that is tomorrow I say
And surely it will come fast

For yesterdays were once todays
that since have come and left
And there's only so many tomorrow days
until you're out of breath

So I pray it's not my last today for what a day it's been
And truly hope tomorrow then becomes today again.

## 2. Rope Finger Man

I mess up when holding hands
I try with all I've got
But when you have rope fingers
It always ends up in a knot

I played patty cake long ago
I got tangled up for hours
My hands get stuck up in my hair
When I shampoo in the shower

One time a boy fell in a well
So deep no one could reach though
Good thing I have rope fingers
Cause now people call me a hero.

| / |
| / |
| / |
| / |
| / |
| / |
| / |
| / |

### 3. Down the Drain
I nearly went down the drain today
Right down in the hole
The water nearly dragged me down
I could've been swallowed whole

I nearly went down the drain today
Good thing it's very small
Only my big toe went in
But it could've been my all

I nearly went down the drain today
I escaped though in the end
It seems that all I had to do
Was put the plug back in.

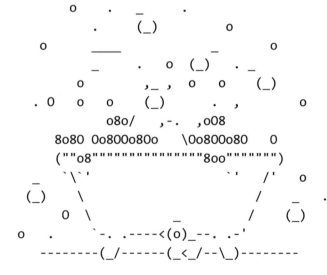

#### 4. Time Isn't Everything

If I could trap time in a bottle
I promise I'd use it for good
I'd give my Mom a few more years
And give my children all I could

I'd tie the bottles in beautiful ribbon
I'd tie them up in silky bows
I'd give a lot of them away as gifts
Or sell them in traveling shows

Perhaps they'd call me *Father Time*
As they came to see my face
In the hopes to get a bottle from me
Wrapped up in pretty lace

But all the people I had seen
Would eventually fall away
As I couldn't give time to everyone
To live another day

Then I'd sit alone with all my time
With nothing left but me
And realize that time isn't everything
But the people within it, you see.

```
+====+
|(::)|
| )( |
|(..)|
+====+
```

### 5. Can A Can Can A Man
A can can can a man
If a man could fit a can
Or if the can could fit a man
A can can can a man, man.

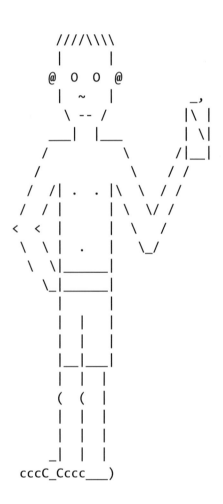

## 6. My Teacher is an Alien

My teacher is an alien
All the kids and I agree
We think we saw her spaceship
Outside during P.E.

We're not a hundred percent
But there are surely warning signs
Perhaps it is her greenish skin
Or the fact she has three eyes

Her antennas draw attention
Her claws clamp and curl
All the kids and I agree
Our teacher might be out of this world.

```
                           . - .
        . - " " " ` " " - .      | (@ @)
    _/ ` oOoOoOoOo ` \_   \  \-/
  ' . -=-=-=-=-=-=- . '    \/  \
    ` -=.=-.-=.=- '         \  /\
        ^   ^   ^            _H_
```

### 7. My Nothing

I went to Nothing Mart today
And I bought me not a thing
I spent nothing on it
But the register went *KA-CHING*

I took it home and put it down
Right next to my favorite playset
But I can't find my nothing now
It seems I have misplaced it.

```
  _aiS########Cms_
 _A##A@"" ""9S##Ss_
c###S            R####s
"^^"             S####
                r###S
             _s###@S
         _cS##@s
       rS###S"
      s###S
      c###s
      r###s
      c###s
      "SS#'


      ____
     a###s
      """
```

### 8. Garbage Bin

I hid inside my garbage bin
To try and see where trash goes
I got picked up by a big green truck
Then we drove down some back roads

It dropped me off on a mountain
Of things people had tossed away
Moldy cheese, scratched CDs
And half eaten fish filets

Old used tires, broken fryers
Water bottles galore
The trash dump had everything
And I think maybe more

I strung together soda cans
I stacked up boxes and bags
I built myself a castle
Out of jam jars and old rags

I ruled the dump with an iron fist
I was a mighty mighty king
Although my subjects were popped balloons
With bodies of paper and string

Eventually someone noticed me
And drove me way back home
My kingdom had finally come an end
A lot like back in Rome

I came home smelling funky
My parents asked me where I'd been
That's when I had to tell them
I hid inside the garbage bin.

```
   _.+._
(^\/^\/^)
 \@*@*@/
 {_____}
```

## 9. A Tornado Took My Cow
A tornado took my cow today
But I quickly caught a break
It turned around and brought her back
But now she makes milkshakes.

```
\\\\\\\\\\\\\\\\\\\\\\\\\\\\\\\\\\\\\\\\
 \\\\\\\\\\\\\\\\\\\\\\\\\\\\\\\\\\\\\\\
  \\\\\\\\\\\\\\\\\\\\\\\\\\\\\\\\\\\\\
   \\\\\\\\\\\\\\\\\\\\\\\\\\\\\\\\\\
    \\\\\\\\\\\\\\\\\\\\\\\\\\\\\\\
     \\\\\\\\\\\\\\\\\\\\\\\\\\
      \\\\\\\\\\\\\\\\\\\\\
       \\\\\\\\\\\\\\\\
       \\\\\\\\\\\\\\
       \\\\\\\\\\\\
      \\\\\\\\\\\\\
      \\\\\\\\\\\\\
      \\\\\\\\\\\\
      \\\\\\\\\\\\
      \\\\\\\\\\\\
 `    \\\\\\\\\\\\          `      `
    *     \\\\\\\\\\\\    *     *
 `    *    *   \\\\\\\\\\\\\    *   *    `
      *    *    \\\\\\\\\\\    *
 `      *    * \\\\\\\\\\ *    *      `
 `    `    *   \\\\\\\\    *    `_____
      \ \ \ * \\\\\\\   * /  /\``````\
      \ \ \ \ \\\\\\  / / / / \``````\
   \ \ \ \ \ \\\\\\\ / / / /  |[] | []|
```

## 10. Pillow Fight

I got upset and punched my pillow
And I wouldn't make this up
The pillow stood up and hit me back
So I kicked him in his fluff

He jumped in the air and landed down
Smacking me upon my head
So I grabbed him by his waist
And threw him right off of the bed

I leaped off of the mattress
And dropped on him with my elbow
I wonder if this is a pillow fight
Or if I'm just fighting my pillow

I pinned him down and counted out
One, two, three I screamed
Then I woke up sprawled out on the floor
Oh dear, I must have dreamed.

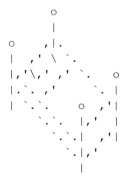

## 11. UsedKeyboard

I-Bought-A-Used-Keyboard,I_Got_It_For_A_Steal,I/Paid/A/Dollar/For/It
,It*Sounded*Like*A*Deal,When(I)Got(Back)Home,I'Plugged'It'In'To'See
,If~It~Would~Even~Work,Without{A}Space{Or}Enter{Key}.

```
,-----------------------------------------------------,
I  [][][][][]   [][][][][]   [][][][]   [][__]   [][][][]  I
I                                                          I
I   [][][][][][][][][][][][][][][_]       [][][]  [][][][] I
I   [_][][][][][][][][][][][][][][ I       [][][]  [][][][] I
I   [][_][][][][][][][][][][][][][]II      []      [][][][] I
I   [__][][][][][][][][][][][][][_]      [][][]  [][][]|| I
I     [__]                    [__]       [][][]  [__][]|| I
`-----------------------------------------------------'
```

## 12. I Don't Know

I don't know the ending to this
As I have yet to write it yet
But the end is coming soon
That I would have to bet

This is another stanza
Which is just a group of lines
Often seen in poetry
A lot like you see in mine

This is the end of the poem
What do you expect?
Do you think that it will rhyme?
Pterodactyl.

¯\_(ツ)_/¯

### 13. Skydiver

I jumped from a plane
My arms spread out wide
The wind whipped through my hair
And wooshed by my side

People said I'd never do it
I heard them laugh and scoff
Especially when I hit the ground
Since I jumped before take off.

```
              . -~~~-.
       .- ~ ~-(       )_ _
      /                    ~ -.
     |                          \
      \                          .'
       ~-  . _____  . -~


               . -~~~-.
        .- ~ ~-(       )_ _
       /                    ~ -.
      |                          \
       \                          .'
        ~-  . _____  . -~
```

## 14. Winter

I turned the knob on the AC
I left open the freezer
I turned on every ceiling fan
I'll make tomorrow winter

I'll wake up to fresh powder
Up and down my icey stairs
They'll be icicles on my showerhead
And snow piled in my chairs

I'll make sure well before bedtime
That I leave on the kitchen sink
So tomorrow I can strap on skates
In a homemade hockey rink

Maybe I'll make snow angels
Down in front of the TV
Who cares if it's July
It's wintertime to me.

```
                              _ _
                            (_) `,
                             ) ,'.\
                             \ ._(
                           ,')`='.
                           `,',' .(|
    ,'_____,',,-,--..._(;(`._.|)
   ///  //\\ ((((       `',`-,-'
  ((_`_-\\-_`_))' _    ,'.,'\_\,.
 ._,-`----------'-.'  `-..\_(_.-\_,'`._
```

## 15. T-Rex Chicken

My chicken hatched a t-rex
Right out there in the coop
He had a scaly tail
And those tiny arms to boot

He thought he was a chicken
Though his teeth were sharp as knives
The other chickens feared him
And all ran for their lives

He chased them just to play
Though his cluck was more a roar
He grew to big to fit his nest
So he slept on the coop floor

Then he got to big for the coop
So he had to stay outside
Still his mommy chicken loved him so
No matter how tall or wide

But he needed to be with other dinosaurs
So I built him a time machine
And sent my T-Rex chicken
Back to eighty million B.C.

## 16. Laser Eye Surgery

So I was disappointed today
After my laser eye surgery
But a lawyer said I couldn't sue
So there will be no judge or jury

I can see fine don't get me wrong
I see better now than ever
But I can't shoot lasers from my eyes
So things could still be better.

```
                    _____
            .-=d88888888888b=-.
          .:d8888pr"|\|/-\|'rq8888b.
        ,:d8888P^//\-\/_\ /_\/^q888/b.
       ,;d88888/~-/ .-~  _~-. |/-q88888b,
      //8888887-\ _/    (#)   \\-\/Y88888b\
      \8888888|// T      `      Y _/|888888 o
       \q88888|- \l            !\_/|88888p/
        'q8888l\-//\          / /\|!8888P'
         'q888\/-| "-,___.-^\/-\/888P'
          `=88\./-/|/ |-/!\/-!/88='
            ^^"_____"^
```

## 17. I Hope You Have A Magnifying Glass

This is the smallest that I could type
Smaller than a crumb
I bet that if you tried
You could cover this with your thumb

I hope you have a magnifying glass
You likely can't read this without one
But if you do hello to you
I appreciate your dedication.

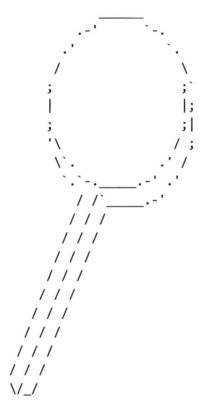

## 18. How's the Future

Right now you're reading this
But I'm back in the past
Although it's new and now to you
Our distances are vast

How's the future treating you?
Did we make it up to Mars?
Are the robots running things now?
Do we all drive flying cars?

Who knows how far in the future
You are to have made it here
All I know is where I am right now
And I know it isn't there.

## 19. Calling In

I called in sick to work today
They hung up in my face
Probably cause I'm unemployed
And it wasn't my workplace.

```
                    _____
              .'  /  /    )
             /   /##/    /|
            /   `--'    / |
           /__ __ __ / |
          //_//_//_//  /
          //_//_//_//  /
          //_//_//_//  /
          //_//_//_//  /
         /          /  /
        /   .-.   /  /
       /   /#/  /  /
      /   `-'  /  /
     / .====.  /  /
    |`-------'  /
     \   ,    .'
      `-//----'
       //
       //
      (())
      (())
      (())
      (())
```

## 20. Flushed

Mom flushed my favorite goldfish
While I stood by and cried
He swirled around then went straight down
Just like a water slide

I thought It looked like lots of fun
To that I had no doubt
So one night I stepped inside the toilet
And flushed it to find out

The bathroom is a mess now
My PJs got all soaked
I fell out of the toilet
I slipped on a bar of soap

I pulled the shower curtain down
And the rod came with it too
I hit my head on the bathroom sink
And now I'm black and blue.

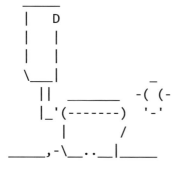

## 21. The Curious Case of Ted the Sub Sandwich

Ted stapled french bread to his chest
On his back he had some stitched
He screamed at random strangers
*"I'm Ted the Sub Sandwich!"*

Everyone in town ignored
And often avoided Ted
Outsiders have asked us why
But it was pretty much the bread

Ted the Sub Sandwich man
Often put pickles in his pocket
He walked around with honey mustard
And cheese stuffed in his wallet

So goes the curious case
Of Mister Sub Sandwich Ted
The man who bathes in mayonnaise
And sleeps in a lettuce bed.

```
       ___
    .'o 0'-._
   / 0 o_.-`|
  /0_.-'  0 |
  | o   o .-`
  |o 0_.-'
  '__`
```

## 22. The Chemist
The chemist ran a marathon
Twenty six miles street side
Then after he crossed the finish
He downed Dihydrogen Monoxide.

### 23. Investment

I invested in storks
Now I have more than a flock
They flap around my living room
All day and night they squawk

Oh, if only I had better ears
Then maybe I'd of heard
They said to invest in *STOCKS*...
Not in a ton of birds.

### 24. Peter's Paper Airplane

Peter made a paper airplane
On his roof with a thousand sheets
He taped and glue and folded
Outside in the summer heat

The paper airplane had paper wings
That stretched out twenty feet
Peter built a paper cockpit too
And rows of paper seats

Peter made a paper pilot
Paper peanuts in paper bags
He made a paper traffic controller
Who wove with paper flags

Peter pushed the paper airplane
Off his roof into the sky
And traveled around the world
In a paper airplane that could fly.

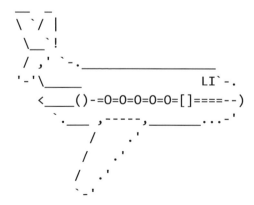

### 25. Robbed

My house was robbed last night
I think but I'm not clear
Cause they only took my TV remote
And my favorite underwear

I'm also missing a penny
From my little piggy bank
And somehow they stole an ounce of water
Right from my fish's tank

I'm missing something else too
I can't remember what or where
Maybe they took my memories
All I know is that it was here

Lastly they took the top button
From my nicest fanciest shirt
And I'm pretty sure the burglars
Ate my leftover dessert.

### 26. This

This is this
And that was that
And this is was
Cause now were at

But now were not
Cause now were here
And here is different
It isn't there

Cause there we were
It didn't last
And now is gone
It's in the past.

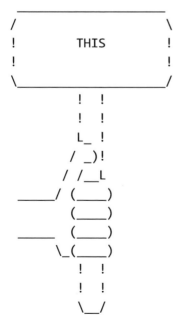

## 27. Super Store

I went to my local Superstore
Which is a really misleading phrase
There were no capes or costumes
No radiation or gamma rays

All there was were stupid groceries
Stacked up on shelves just right
And though I walked the entire store
There were no super villains to fight

I guess I'll find my powers elsewhere
It seems I'll just keep looking
Until then I should grab some bread
'Cause the loaf at home is molding.

```
            .=.,
           ;c =\
         __|  _/
       .'-'-._/-'-._
      /..        ___     \
     /'  _   [<_->] )   \
    (   / \--\_>/-/'._  )
     \-;_/\__;__/ _/ _/
      '._}|==o==\{_\/
       /  /-._.--\  \_
      // /   /|   \ \ \
     / | |   | \;  |  \ \
    / /  |  :/   \: \   \_\
   /  |  /.'|   /: |    \ \
   |  |  |--| . |--|     \_\
   / _/  \ | : | /___--._) \
  |_(---'-| >-'-| |        '-'
        /_/      \_\
```

## 28. Tickolus Tock
Oh, Tickolus Tock
Lived in a big clock
Why? No one really knew
But from his tower
After every hour
He peaked out and screamed,"*CUCKOO!!!*"

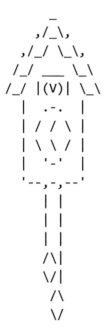

### 29. Cap'n Dan

Dan's not a good pirate captain
He only sails one sea
His ship is often leaky
And his cabin's infested with fleas

His cannons don't quite work
And neither does his lazy crew
They lay around the shipdeck all day
When there are pirate things to do

"Ship on the horizon!" Cap'n Dan yelled,
"It's time to be a pirate!"
That's when the crew looked out and said
"Nah, we don't feel like it."

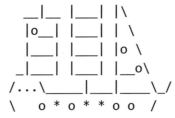

## 30. Collecting My Thoughts

I collected all my thoughts
And kept them in glass cases
Some of them were silly
And some were familiar faces

There's so many, I built a museum
I broke it into sections
To the left are my favorite holidays
To the right are recollections

In the basement you'll find my darkest fears
Upstairs, the wildest dreams
In the heart shaped room there are things I love
Like those cookies with the cream

Out there, the garden holds my trips
And vacations to far away places
But only I can visit my museum
Of my thoughts caught in glass cases

There is a room that I avoid though
It's got thoughts that make me sad
A room of things that I have lost
And thoughts that make me mad

I do go there from time to time
Cause it's fine to feel that way
But then I look for my happy things
And it helps it go away.

```
          _ - - -~~(~~-_.
       _{             )   )
   ,      ) -~~- ( ,-' )_
   (   `-,_..`.,  )-- '_,)
   ( `  _)  (  -~( -_ `,  }
   (_-  _  ~_-~~~~`,  ,' )
     `~ -^(    __;-,(((())))
       ~~~~ {_ -_(())
            `\  }
```

## 31. Dog Walker

Walter is a dog walker
You've probably seen him before
He's the one that walks through town
Trotting on all fours

He pees on fire hydrants
He barks when people pass
Worst of all, he eats dog food
Which gives him awful gas.

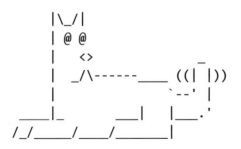

## 32. Mirror

I put a mirror on the ground
And faced it toward the sky
Now when I look down
I see clouds that pass me by

I think if you're not careful
You could fall down and through
And falling would mean going up
Forever through the blue

I tried it out and dropped a ball
It fell out of my sight
"It's real" I yelled "It's really real"
That's not possible right?

I stepped back to take a moment
To absorb what I'd just said
That's when a ball came crashing down
And struck me in my head.

```
                 ____
           .:::---:::.
        .'--:        :--'.
      /.'     \   /     `.\
     | /'._  /:::\  _.'\ |
     |/      |:::::|     \|
     |:\ .''-:::-''. /:|
      \:|    `|`    |:/
       '.'._.:::._.'.'
        '-:::::::-'
```

### 33. Alarm Clock

My alarm clock has bad memory
It's the worst thing I've ever bought
I tell it to wake me but then I'm late
Cause the clock says he forgot.

```
         . - . - .
(( (__I__) ))
   .'_....._'.
  / / .12 . \ \
 | | '  |  ' | |
 | | 9  /  3 | |
  \ \ '.6.' / /
   '.`-...-'.'
    /'-- --'\
   ` " " " " " " " " " "`
```

### 34. My Chair Has Legs

My chair has legs my chair has legs
And I'm not fast enough to match them
Good thing my fridge is running
So I asked if he could catch him

So there we were the two of us
Chasing chair across the street
That's when I saw my sofa too
Man! I forgot that he had feet.

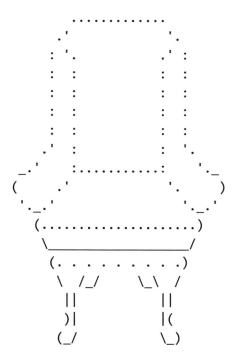

## 35. The Mermaid

I think I saw a mermaid once
While swimming in the sea
I saw her in the distance waves
I think she waved at me

I had to go so I waved goodbye
Since it was getting dark
On second thought, it may've been a girl
Being eaten by a shark.

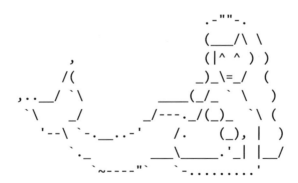

## 36. Magic

I need you to clear your mind for a second
Then just read the words below
Are you ready for some magic?
Close your eyes, picture a rainbow

...

Isn't that simply amazing
The things that you can do
Don't ever wait for magic again
The magical thing is **YOU**.

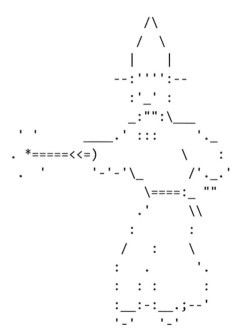

## 37 .Upside Down Day

Happy upside down day
Now be sure not to cheat
Remember to walk with just your hands
And grab things with your feet

Slip your pants on over your head
You can look out through your zipper
Then stick your legs inside your sleeves
Whether it be a t-shirt or a sweater

At noon's the upside down parade
Though it's nothing to promote
The parade doesn't move much at all
Cause the people are under the floats

But night's the upside down firework show
Which is sure to be lots of fun
Just know that if you want to go
You need to know how to run.

```
              .
          .'  |
         .'    |
        /`-._'
       /   /
      /   /
     /   /
    (`-./
     )
     '
```

## 38. This Could Have Been Good
Words can do amazing tricks
They can paint things crystal clear
But not these words and not this poem
Because this one ends right here.

```
_____$$$$
_____$$__$
_____$___$$
_____$___$$
_____$$___$$
_____$____$$
_____$$____$$$
_____$$_____$$
_____$$_____$$
_____$_____$$
____$$$$$$$_____$$
__$$$_____$$$$$$
_$$____$$$$_____$$$
_$___$$$__$$$_____$$
_$$_____$$$_____$
__$$___$$$$$$_____$
__$$$$$$$____$$_____$
__$$_____$$$$_____$
___$$$$$$$$$__$$_____$$
_____$_____$$$$____$$$$
____$$___$$$$$$___$$$$$$
_____$$$$$$____$$__$$
_____$____$$$_$$$
_____$$$$$$$$$$$
```

### 39. Monster Attack

My car was attacked by something today
But by what I do not know
It pounded against the metal doors
It's tentacles slapped my window

It rocked and shook the car around
There were lights that flickered and flashed
I thought that we were doomed for sure
I thought we were gonna crash

It was the largest monster to ever roam
It's roar sounded loud and mean
It covered the car in water and foam
It made the car *squeaky clean!*

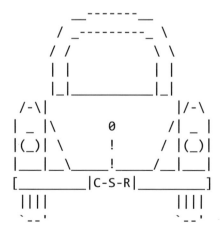

## 40. My Lovest Love
I feel the land where my lovest love lies
Is covered by nothing but the bluest blue skies
And the greenest green grass that ever could grow
That is where my lovest love lies I know

I promise to get there,
Swear-est swear that I will
The soon-est soon that I can
with not a moment to kill

Then I'll stay with them for the ever-est of for
My most lovest love for the forever-est of more.

```
_____$$$$_____$$$$
___$$$$$$$$$_____$$$$$$$$$
_$$$$$$$$$$$$$_$$$$$$$$$$$$$$
$$$$$$$$$$$$$$$$$$$$$$$$$$$$$$$
$$$$$$$$$$$$$CS$$$$$$$$$$$$$$$
_$$$$$$$$$$$$AS$$$$$$$$$$$$$$
__$$$$$$$$$$$$$$$$$$$$$$$$$$
____$$$$$$$$$$$$$$$$$$$$$$
_____$$$$$$$$$$$$$$
_____$$$$$$$
_____$$$
_____$
```

r

## 41. Bags of Breath

Breath, breath, bags of breath for sale
Come buy a wrapped sack filled with my exhale

Use them for parties
Use them for decor
Tie them to your mailboxes
Leave them on the floor

My bags of breath aren't selling, I wonder what's to blame
On second thought I figure… It's probably the name

Maybe I'll call them Airbags
No wait that's already a thing
Maybe I'll call them Puffsacks
Nah, that doesn't have a ring

Perhaps it should be nonsensical,
Just as long as I think of it soon
It doesn't even need to be a real word
Something random like *BALLOON!*

```
____$$$$$$$$$
_$$_____$$
$_____$
$_____$___$$$$$$$$
$_____$_$$_____$$
$_____$$_____$
_$_____$$_$_____$
__$$$____$$$__$_____$
_____$$$$_____$_____$
_____$$_____$_____$$
_____$$_____$$$____$$
_____$$_____$$$$
_____$_____$$
_____$_____$$
_____$$_____$$
_____$$_____$
_____$$_____$
_____$_____$$
_____$_____$$
_____$_____$
```

## 42. Under Construction
This poem is under construction
Words may need to be rearranged
Come back later and who knows
Maybe something will have changed.

## 43. Upside Down

I hope you don't get mad at me
Please don't fret or frown
But it seems I accidentally printed
This poem upside down

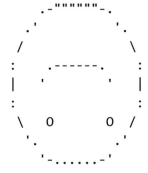

### 44. Frank the Goldfish

A fish out of water, how absurd the thought.
Yet Frank the goldfish tried with all that he got
.He swam to the bottom of his little water bowl
And with belly on the rocks he imagined his goal
Frank swam to the top then flipped through the sky
Yelling as loud as he could, "Frank the Goldfish can fly!"
He flew through the kitchen, Yes, Frank was a winner
Then he landed in my pan, looks like seafood for dinner!

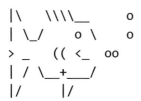

## 45. Snow

*"Don't eat yellow snow"*
I think we've all been told these words
But no one had even told me once
That chocolate snow is worse.

```
_____,¯.___          _
|____            { {]_]_]    [_]
|___   `-----.__\ \_]_]_       . `
|    `-----.____} }]_]_]_      ,
|_____/ {_]_]_]_] , `
```

### 46. Take Whisks

Utensils sound blunt
And silverware isn't great
A spoon or fork is boring
On the side of your plate

So do something different
It's nice to take risks
How 'bout tonight you try eating
Your soup with a whisk

Be odd, it's fine and know deep inside
That there are no rights or wrongs
And next time you're eating some mac and cheese
Try busting out the tongs.

### 47. Thank You

Your soft touch on my cheek
The way you tend to me when I'm sick
You take the blows I deal you
You're there through thin and thick

I wish I knew how to say thanks
For all of the things that you do
You truly are an amazing thing
Rectangular box of tissues.

## 48. Football

A question just popped in my head
"What shape would you call a football?"
I thought and thought and thought
But I can't remember or recall

It's kind of roundish right?
But also pointy on the ends
Sort of like a circle
But also like pyramids

I couldn't quite figure it out
And I was getting pretty annoyed
So I searched "football shape" on the web
It's a *Prolate Spheroid*.

```
                   __
             .-'||||'-.
           .'     ||     '.
          /     _||_      \
         | /`-       -`\ |
         | | 6      6 | |
          \/\___7___/\/
    .--------:\:I:II:I:/;--------.
   /          \`:I::I:`/          \
  |             `------'           |
  |              \___/             |
  |    ,      __    ___     ,      |
  |======|   / / /  _  \  |======|
  |======|  / /__ \ <_> /  |======|
  |~~~~~|  | <_> \/ <_> \  |~~~~~|
  |     |\  \___/\___/  /|      |
   \   \/                |/    /
    `\    \ _ _.-=""=-._ _ /    /'
      `\   '`_)\\-++++-//(_`'   /'
       ;   (__||    ||__)   ;
       ;    ___\    /___    ;
       '.  ---/-=..=-\--- .'
```

## 49. Into the Screen

I fell into my phone today
Into the screen I went
I landed on an app
That opened messages I sent

I climbed up all the chat bubbles
Until I reached the top
Then I saw my contacts
And into them I hopped

I tried to call for help
But people thought it was a joke
Like I was just crank calling
Or someone out there blowing smoke

So I hiked to listen to music
From an app that keeps my songs
I listened to my favorite ones
I even sang along

Then I dove into to social media
And posted up a plea
All I got was a couple likes
Well exactly twenty three

After awhile I skipped on over
To watch some videos on an app
And after a couple hours of them
I decided to take a nap

When I woke up, I was outside the screen
My nightmare had come to an end
Then after a moment, I picked up my phone
And fell inside again.

```
 ___
|   |
|   |
|_o_|
```

## 50. Sherlack Hams

Sherlack Hams was the worst detective
He could barely gather clues
Once we saw him tracking prints
He'd made with his own shoes

Though he tried his very best
Sherlack had never solved a case
Even if the all the answers
Sat directly in his face

Sherlack often dusted for prints
But he'd cover the room in powder
Police would try to preserve the scene
But Sherlack would spill his chowder

Sherlack always had a hunch
He was always follow and trailing
But Sherlack Hams was the worst detective
Or the best detective at failing.

## 51. Chicken Fried Kitchen

Chicken fried chicken fried
Chicken fried steak
In the *Chicken Fried Kitchen*
Chicken fried whatever it could bake

Chicken fried french fries
Chicken fried tots
Chicken fried pot pies
Chicken fried pots

Chicken fried breads
Chicken fried fruits
Chicken fried beds
And chicken fried boots

Chicken fried baseballs
Chicken fried bikes
Chicken fried overalls
Chicken fried kites

Chicken fried chicken fried
In the *Chicken Fried Kitchen*
'Til Chicken got carried away
And Chicken fried Chicken.

## 52. Stick Figure Man

I drew a photo once
Of a stick figure man
Near a stick figure house
In a stick figure land

The sun sat up in the corner
With rays of squiggly lines
I think about stick figure man
I hope he's doing fine

I drew him a wife and kids
I drew them a family dog
I drew a pond right near the house
With a lily pad and frog

I drew a path winding down
To the sidewalk and the street
I drew some clouds up in the sky
And neighbors for them to meet

I drew a great big tree and branch
On which the kids would have a swing
I drew V birds near the clouds
So they could hear them sing

I hope that they enjoy their world
The man, his kids and wife
I hope I gave Stick Figure Man
A very happy life.

```
('))  ^v^  _              (`)_
(__)_)  ,--j j-------,  (__)_)
     /_.-.___.-._/ \        o
  ,8|  [_],-.[_]  |  oOo      /|\
,,,oO8|_o8_|_|_8o_|&888o,,,/  \
```

## 53. Name Your Price

Everything has a price
That's what people say
So how much do I need
To see your face every day?

I have a dollar in my wallet
I have a few pennies in a jar
I have a quarter in my pocket
I have a nickel in my car

Name your price
Go on ahead, I'll see what I can do
I just need to know how much I need
To spend my life with you.

```
           _.-'~~`~~'-._
        .'`  B   E   R   `'.
       / I                T \
      /`        .-'~"-.       `\
    ; L       / `-   \        Y ;
    ;        /> `. -.|          ;
    |       /_     '-._)        |
    |      |-  _.' \ |          |
    ;       `~~;    \\          ;
    ;  INGODWE /      \\)       ;
     \  TRUST '.___.-'`"       /
      `\                     /`
        '._   1 9 9 5    _.'
          `'-..,,,,..-'`
```

### 54. Stop It

Mary looked into her mirror
Her face was frozen with fear
The fright so simple a giant pimple
On her cheek so clear

Mary couldn't seem to drop it
So she decided that she'd pop it
She pinched and squeezed and to her unease
The zit told her to stop it.

## 55. Sparkling Water

Sparkling water sounds incredible
It sounds like it could be magic
But then you take a sip to find
It tastes like TV static.

```
           _____
      |   /~~~~~~~~~\  | | |
      | |~~~~~~~~~~~~| . . .|
      | |~~~~~~~~~~~~|     |
      |  _____/   O  |
        ~~~~~~~~~~~~~~~~~~
```

## 56. Put It On

You can put on pants
You can put on shirts
You can put on jackets
Shorts and skirts

You can put on socks
You can put on hats
You can put on shoes
Boots, heels and flats

You can put on whatever
You can pick from the pile
But be sure you remember
To put on your smile.

```
        __   __
  /|  |/|\|  |\
 /_|  ´ |.`  |_\
   |    |.   |
   |    |.   |
   |___|.__|
```

## 57. Shaved

I went and shaved my face today
But I cut a little to close
I mean yeah, it's great my beard is gone
But also so's my nose.

```
_____$
_____$$
_____$$
_____$$$
_____$$$
_____$$$$
_____$$$$
_____$$$$
_____$$$
_____$$
_$$$_____$$
$$_____$$
$$_____$$
$$_____$$$$$$$$_____$$
_$$____$$$$$$$$$$$$$$
__$$$$$$____$$$$$$$$
____$$$____$$
```

## 58. Fishing

I went reverse fishing today
But my Dad wanted to fish right
It's good to do things differently
Though it caused a little fight

I had grabbed my trusty fishing rod
I jumped into the water
Then flung my hook onto the dock
And caught myself a Father.

```
     ,%&& %&& %
    ,%&%& %&%& %&
   %& %&% &%&% % &%
  % &%% %&% &% %&%&,
  &%&% %&%& %& &%& %
 %%& %&%& %&%&% %&%%&
 &%&% %&% % %& &% %%&
 && %&% %&%& %&% %&%'
  '%&% %&% %&&%&%%'%
   % %& %& %&% &%%
     `\%%.'  /`%&'
     |   |           /`-._           _\\/
     |,  |_         /        `-._ ..--~`  _
     |;  |_`\_     /  ,\\.~`    `-._ -  ^
     |;: |/^}__..-,@   .~`    ~      `o ~
     |;: |(____.-'      '.   ~   -      ` ~
     |;: |  \ / `\        //.  -    ^     ~
     |;: |\ /' /\_\_       ~._ _ ~    -//-
     \\/;:   \'--' `---`
      `\\//-\\///
```

## 59. The Limit

The sky is not the limit
The only limit in life is you
Limiting yourself
And all the things that you can do

Not everything is possible though
To that I do agree
But if you put you mind to it
Nearly anything can be

And who knows what out there's possible
Who knows what's really the limit
Eventually maybe you will
When you go out and try to find it.

## 60. Lucky Day

I stepped on a crack in the sidewalk
Gee I hope my mothers okay
Then I walked under a ladder
And a black cat crossed my way

I broke my bathroom mirror this morning
I opened an umbrella indoors
I spilt salt at lunch today
But didn't throw it over my shoulders

Then while walking home I slipped
And fell down a steep hillside
I hit every tree and bush around
It hurt my in and outsides

I came to a stop in a muddy puddle
It was a miracle I was even okay
Then I looked to my right and saw a quarter
Looks like it's my lucky day.

## 61. Puzzle Pieces

I lost a few of my puzzle pieces
Sadly, yes it's true
But I still know my picture
Even though I lost a few

Some were taken away from me
Some got lost along the way
But I still know my picture
And that makes me feel okay

Although you may lose pieces sometimes
It's sad, sadly it's true
Never forget the beautiful picture
Of the puzzle that makes up you.

### 62. Metal Work
My uncle said he did metal work
So I tagged along with him in his car
But I was confused when he grabbed his blow torch
And I had brought my guitar.

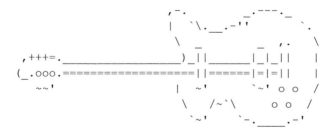

## 63. Homegrown Fantasy

I dug deep into the soil
And planted seeds of dreams
Watered them with imagination
Nourished them under love beams

I watched them daily in my yard
Growing tall for all to see
Just how much I truly cared
About a homegrown fantasy

Then one day I will reap
From which that I had sewn
I'll bundle the fruits of my labor
From the dreams that I had grown

I'll then take them to the local market
And give each of them away
To every lost and lonely person
Looking for a dream that day.

```
           wWWWw                         wWWWw
   vVVVv  (___)  wWWWw              (___)  vVVVv
   (___)   ~Y~   (___)   vVVVv      ~Y~   (___)
    ~Y~    \|     ~Y~    (___)      |/     ~Y~
    \|    \ |/   \| /   \~Y~/      \|     \ |/
    \\|//  \\|// \\|/// \\|//     \\|//  \\\|///
   ^^^^^^^^^^^^^^^^^^^^^^^^^^^^^^^^^^^^^^^^^^^^^
```

## 64. Original Thought Haikus

It's hard to have an original thought
To think something never thought before
You have to think outside the box
And be cunning and clever for sure

It has to be something different
It can weird or something strange
Even if it's slightly off
Or completely out of range

So here we go, lets try it out
Below we have a few
But this is a poetry book of course
So I wrote them in haikus

...

"The circle pancake's
Only impressive during
Level five earthquakes"

"The hoarders house was
So very clean and pristine
Of course I'm kidding"

"If dogs see in gray
Do you think the sky's the same
On cloudy days"

"Once I knew a guy
Who would like to hit the sauce
Ranch went everywhere"

"Cock-eyed brides bouquets
Get thrown in all sorts of ways.
It's their special day."

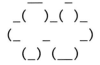

## 65. Anxiety

I went out to a fancy restaurant
To get my favorite dish
A plate of sauteed veggies surrounding
A wonderfully cooked fish

The waiter sat down my plate for me
Then went my greatest fear
To "*Enjoy the food*" I said "*Thanks, you too!*"
I can never come back here.

### 66. Push or Pull

If pushing doesn't work
Then I guess try to pull
But don't you let a silly door
Turn you into a fool

So if pulling doesn't work
I guess it's time to break it down
Go buy a battering ram
And beat it to the ground

But if the ram doesn't work
I guess the door is blocked
I mean, either that or maybe
The door is simply locked.

## 67. I Could Eat You Up

I could just eat you up
I could just swallow you whole
You're so cute I could mash you up
And eat you from a bowl

I could sprinkle you with salts
Or maybe spices would be nifty
Then I'll go heat the oven for you
To something around three fifty

I'll pair you with the finest sides
Set the table, nice as can be
You're so cute I could eat you up
You're just that cute to me.

```
            ( \
             \ \
        __    \ \ ___,.--------..__           __
      //\\ _,-\\              `'--._  //\\
      \\ ;'    \\                  `://
       `(       \\                    )'
        :.       \\,----,          ,;
        `.`--.__\(   /     ___.--','
            `  ``-----'_-''      ,'
          -.            ,-
            `-._____.-'
```

### 68. Killed Time

I killed time the other day
And it's been 10AM since
The sun has sat stuck in the sky
The moon hasn't moved an inch

The police took me from my home
They charged me with the crime
Murder in the first degree
For the tragic killing of time

When I went down to the courthouse
The judge said I was in denial
"I didn't mean to kill time I swear!"
I shouted during my trial

I can't believe this is happening
I thought time was always my friend
But now that I've killed time
It seems it won't happen again.

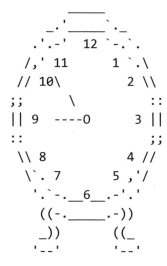

## 69. Delicious, Delectable

I took a bite off of my fork
In my brain I started to scream
So delicious! So delectable!
It tastes just like a dream!

So flavorsome! So succulent!
So lusciously mouthwatering!
The most delightful, most savory!
Most heavenly appetizing!

Oh my how tasty! Me oh my!
My how lovely and divine!
My how exquisite! Wow, so rich!
My how gloriously delish!

With a gulp I swallowed the bite
And sent it down into my tummy
Then when I could finally muster words
All I managed to say was *"yummy!"*

### 70. Terry Teeter Vegetable Eater

Terry Teeter, Vegetable Eater
Ate all his veggies with haste
Every carrot, every broccoli
He'd have to have a taste

Nothing beat a beet to Terry
And nothing was ahead of lettuce
There were no spare asparagus to eat
We asked him, he wouldn't let us

Terry Teeter, Vegetable Eater
Ate every crunchy green and root
That there wasn't a single thing left for us
Except for all the fruit.

71. Mind Control (Read Aloud)
Author transmission, begin operation
Signal loud and clear
Subject secure. Message C49
The poem will begin here:

So each of these letters creates a thought
A thought that enters my mind
And I now say anything the author wants
As long as I'm reading these lines

Peanut butter popsicles
Yesterday's moldy cheese
My name is Ephram Stefagopolis
May I have a lamp post please

I have an itchy buttox
I also have fingers that stink
I own a purple elephant named Bill
I drive a car thats pink

Oh my, see what I mean
I'll say whatever is written down
Hmm… I wonder if I'll do other things
After this line, I'm going to frown :(

!!!NOW I AM SCREAMING!!!
Now I'm speaking in a whisper
Now I'm going to sound like a cat (*Meeowww*)
Watch me twirl and twist my whiskers

I will now close one eye and speak like a pirate
*ARRRRG I SAIL THE SEVEN SEAS*
Now here is an alright impression
Of a buzzing little bee! (*Bzzz Bzzz Bzzz*)

Okay, I'm done, stop reading now
Reassign subject to role
Signal fading, cease transmission
BEEP! End of mind control.

01000011 00100000 00100000 01010011 00100000 00100000
01010010 00100000 00101101 00100000 01001001 00100000
00100000 01001100 00100000 00100000 01011001

## 72. Thanks Arachnophobia

A spider crawled into my bathtub
It stopped by to say hello
Shout out arachnophobia
For turning my bath water yellow.

```
      ____                            ,
    /---.'.__                  ____//
       '--.\              /.---'
   _____   \\          //
  /.------.\   \|       .'/    _____
 //    __   \ \  ||/|\   //   _/_----.\__
 |/  /.-.\   \ \:|< >|// _/.'..\    '--'
   //    \'.  | \'.|.'/ /_/ /  \\
   //      \ \_\/" ' ~\-'.-'      \\
  //         '-._|  :H:  |'-.__      \\
 //              (/'==='\)'-._\      ||
 ||                          \\     \|
 ||                           \\     '
 |/                            \\
                                ||
                                ||
                                \\
                                 '
```

## 73. Batteries

Zinc carbon or chloride
Oxy nickel hydroxide
Double and triple and AAAA
C and D and even J
F, N, nine or four point fives
Zinc air, mercury and silver oxides
CR's and SR's and A23's
This is a list of batteries.

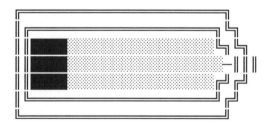

## 74. Silence Is Golden

I think since silence is golden
You should hold onto your tongue
Then wait until the moment
You're 'bout to spit some platinum.

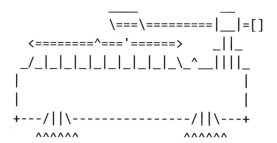

## 75. Halloween

Tis' the night of Halloween
And I got so scared I could shout
A monster gripped onto my face
When I put my mask on inside out.

```
                    /}
         _,---~-LJ,-~-._
      ,-^    '    '    '     ^:,
    :     .      '       '        :
   :     /|  .   /\    '        :
  :   . //|     // \    '      :
  :     `~` /|  `^~`    '       ;
  :   '    //|           '     :
  :    \-_   `~`       ,    '  :
  ;  . \.\_,--,_;^/    ,      :
   :     ^-_!^!__/^    ,     :
    :,  ,  .        ,      :
      ^--_____    .    ;`
            `^''____`
```

## 76. Triceratopses Don't Tip Toe

Triceratopses don't tip toe
They stomp and shake the ground
They headbutt things with mighty force
They weigh twelve thousand pounds

Triceratopses don't tip toe
They aren't really careful at all
They will smash your dad's television set
They will pop your favorite ball

Triceratopses don't tip toe
They take up the entire bed
They don't share the covers at night
So you'll sleep in a sweater instead

Triceratopses don't tip toe
They break things by design
But what can I say, I love this one
Cause this triceratop's mine.

## 77. Dogpile

Dogpiles sound adorable
They sound so cute and sweet
Until you're actually in one
And get kicked by a cleat

Either that or maybe your walking
Then without the slightest clue
You step right into a dogpile
And it sticks onto your shoe

Why can't they be piles of puppies
How fun would that be, just think
Why are most dogpiles athletes
Or mounds of stuff that stink.

Acronyms can be a lot of fun
And *SCUBA* is probably one of the best
The letters stand for **S**elf **C**ontained
**U**nderwater **B**reathing **A**pparatus

What's even cooler is *LASER*
Which is quite the declaration
It's **L**ight **A**mplification by **S**timulated
**E**mission of **R**adiation.

```
                        )    0
                       (   o . 0
                        )   () .
                       /  0   o
                     _.|._  o .()
        _              / _:_ \
     <_><)          |.(_"_).|
        __           _\. : ./_
     |><_'>    / |..:..| \
              /_/ `---' \_\              ,
     ,  (.   \_)           \_)  \)-<
     _) \)~    \  T  /     ,(_)
     _/ -(-<     _)__|__(_    \_)-<~
     \)~ )-<  /....|....\  .~(_,_
     >(_ (_/   """"" """""      _\
     `-.__)__\_.----'`-._____.-'   `-.__
```

### 79. I Was Here

Earth, June Tenth, Twenty-Twenty-One
I leave this as proof I was here
If you're reading this then I was not forgotten
Well phew... That was my fear.

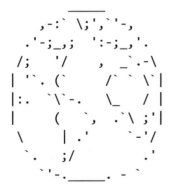

## 80. Flat

The earth isn't flat but pizza is
and it should stay that way
Cause putting toppings on a ball of dough
Is just frustrating, okay...

```
              _.....__
          _.:`.--|--.`:._
        .: .'\o  | o /'. '.
      // '.  \ o|  /  o '.\
     //'._o'. \ |o/ o_.-'o\\
     || o '-.'.\|/.-' o .`||
     ||--o--o-->|<-o--o--o||
```

## 81. My Favorite Subscriber

Hey guys, welcome back to my channel
What's up, welcome back to the stream
Be sure to like, subscribe and follow
Waste time in front of a screen

Watch me become your center
Give into strategies of retention
Or maybe go become something yourself
And give your own life some attention

Your world could be entertaining too
Something worth watching outside of the cyber
Then at the end of the day you can lay down and say
Goodnight, my favorite subscriber.

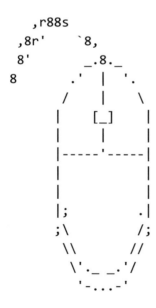

## 82. Most Dangerous Toilet

I built the world's most dangerous toilet
Made of broken glass and glue
Number one was pretty easy
The problem is number two.

```
  .----------------.
  ;----------------;
  |  ~~  .------.    |
  |    /        \    |
  |   /          \   |
  |  |            |  |   ,-----.
  |   \ ,    , /  |  =|_____|=
  '---,########,---'    (---(
     /##'    '##\        )---)
     |##,    ,##|        (---(
      \'######'/         '---`
       \`""""`/
        |`""`|
      .-|    |-.
     /  '    '  \
     '----------'
```

### 83. Knock on Wood

When you say a bad thing will happen
Knock on glass or knock on wood
I'm not really sure quite why we do that
I just know when you do, you should

So knock on glass or knock on wood
Bad things may happen unless
You dispel whatever curses may come
By knocking on stuff I guess.

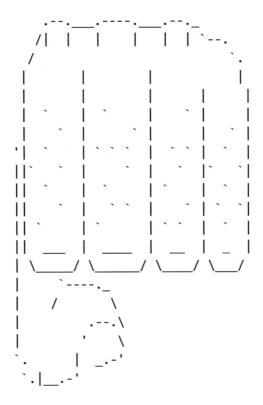

## 84. Hannukah Bush

Living in a mixed religion home is odd
And that's really the only thing I can say
I mean, not many kids opened gifts from the Hanukkah bush
Early Christmas day

I also doubt they had passover dinner
Days before egg hunting on Easter
They probably haven't been to both temple and church
Or tasted matzo ball soup either

Living in a mixed religion home is odd
And that's really the only thing I can say
Not many kids get to grow up like that
But I wouldn't want it any other way.

```
                              __
      __   __   __   __    \__/    __   __   __   __
   \__/\__/\__/\__/   )(   \__/\__/\__/\__/
   )(   )(   )(   )(     )(     )(   )(   )(   )(
   )(   )(   )(    \\__)(__//    )(   )(   )(
   )(    \\   \\    `--)(--'    //   //    )(
    \\    \\    \\____)(____//   //    //
     \\    \\    `-----)(-----'   //    //
      \\    \_____)(_____//    //
       \\     `-------)(-------'   //
        \_____)(_____//
         `----------)(.---------'
                    )(
                   _/\_
                   >()<
                   \/
                   )(
                   (())
            ___.-"^^"-.___
            '==============`
```

### 85. So Much More
I don't know most things to know
Most thing I do not know
I know the things I know mostly
Cause someone told me so

And I won't know most things to know
Most things I will not know
No matter how much I try to learn
There'll be so much more to go.

```
  ( \
   \ ' \
    \ ' \
   / ' |        _____
   \ ' /      ()_____)
      \         \  ~~~~~~~~  \
       \          \  ~~~~~~    \
     (==)          _____\
     (__)        ()_____)
```

<u>86. Someone Just Like___</u>
I have trouble finishing _____
I don't know what to __
I think perhaps that maybe
I need someone just like ___.

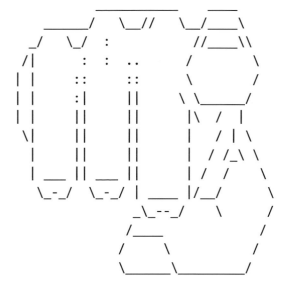

### 87. Rest Assured

Rest assured I rested, sure
I slept the night away
"Good morning everybody"
I yawn and try to say

Rest assured I rested, sure
I need a coffee or frappe
Even more than that perhaps
I think I need a nap.

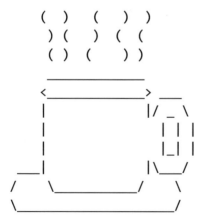

## 88. Million Dollar Idea

I've got a million dollar idea
That one day will buy me a jet
It seems there's only one problem though
I haven't quite thought of it yet

But just you wait cause when I do
You won't believe your eyes
I know I've got a million dollar idea
But what it is, is a surprise.

```
 -----------------------------------
|#######===================#######|
|#(1)*UNITED STATES OF AMERICA*(1)#|
|#**          /===\   *******   **#|
|*# {G}      | (") |           #*|
|#*  *2016*  | /v\ |    O N E    *#|
|#(1)         \===/          (1)#|
|##=====ONE MILLION DOLLARZ======##|
 -----------------------------------
```

## 89. Reverse Vampires

Reverse vampires would be beneficial
They would be helpful not dangers
Cause when they'd get a little hungry
They would donate their blood to strangers.

## 90. Ode to a Post It Note

Post-it note, oh Post-it note
Your sticky strip is great
And everytime I use one of you
There is another lying in wait

You're there for all my random notes
That need not a sheet of paper
But just the simplest of things
Like reminders for me later

"Have a good day at school today!"
"Track meet at five o' clock!"
"Don't forget your lunch sweetie!"
"Take the dog out for a walk!"

What would life be without you Post-Its
I think it'd be pretty rough
Well either that or maybe we'd just
Write on other stuff.

```
 /_____/`-.
<()>_____<   ##>
 \/_____\,-'
```

## 91. When Life Gives You Lemons

"When life gives you lemons, you make lemonade!"
Has been heard by every son and daughter
I've never been given lemons but I've seen rain
So I think I'll make bottled water.

```
            _____
         | _ _ _ _ _ |
         |_____|
          )_____(
         (_____)
         /           \
       /~~~~~~~~~~~~~~\
       /               \
      /                 \
     /                   \
    /                     \
  (_____)
    )_____(
  (_____)
   |                     |
   |_____|
     )_____(
   |_____|
     )_____(
   |                     |
   |_____|
     )_____(
   |_____|
     )_____(
   |                     |
   |                     |
   |_____|
  (_____)
   |_____|
  (_____)
   |                     |
   |                     |
   _____/
    '_____'
```

## 92. Parents Aren't Perfect

Parents aren't perfect
They are people like you
They make mistakes, they get things wrong
At times they can feel blue

And parents aren't perfect
Though they do the things they can
They are just a little girl and boy
Who're now a woman and man

And parents aren't perfect
After times both good and bad
The woman and that man
Became a mother and a dad

And parents aren't perfect
Sometimes they can fall apart
See, they know they aren't perfect
But they love you with all their heart

You may want to see parents as perfect
Though I can promise you they're not
But for a perfect kid like you they'll try
With everything they've got.

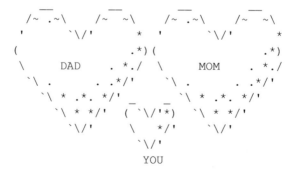

## 93. Shadow in the Mist
A dense fog fell on the street
The moon faded from sight
All I could see was my feet
And the dim glow of a streetlight

Another figure came into view
A shadow out there in the mist
I felt in my heart it must be you
A love that I had missed

I moved so quickly, a haste in my stride
With thoughts of long nights and small talks
I shut my eyes tight, held my arms out wide
Then realized I hugged a mailbox.

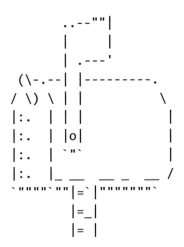

### 94. Gary the Turtle

Gary the turtle moved oh so slow
"Fast!" He said, "That's how I wanna go!"
So his little friend Timmy strapped a rocket to his shell
And one lit fuse later, well, it didn't go well

He soared past cars, he breezed past birds
How fast was this turtle? There were no words
But Gary the turtle was as fast as could be
Until CRASH! He plowed right into a tree.

### 95. Not Myself Today
I am not myself today
Well who am I? I cannot say
Then what am I? I guess okay
But I am not myself today

So who am I? I do not know
I don't think Jason, John or Joe
A similar looking figure though
But in the end I do not know

So what am I? I had say okay
Just having one of those not myself days
I feel different in one of those not myself ways
So I guess I'm just not myself today.

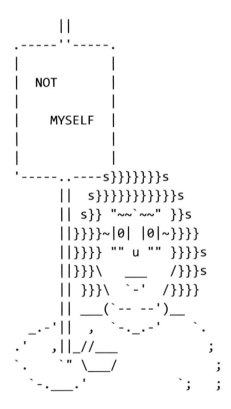

## 96. Even If Dreams Come True

If I could discover what dreams we're made of
I'd conjure them up every day
I'd make the very wildest come true
And create life in my own way

I'd stop sleeping and build a lab in my basement
With beakers and test tubes galore
And the chemicals of happiness and love
Would fill up all of my drawers

Perhaps they would call me the Dreamcatcher
As people watched in a curious gaze
Combining all my elements of dreams
To awe them and amaze

But one day I'd run out of dreams to dream
And I'd have no plans for tomorrow
I'd lose my passions and aspirations
Then with everything, live in sorrow

Then when I'm left with nothing else to do
I'll have nothing to do but cry
And realize that even if dreams come true
They mean nothing if you didn't try.

```
| - |    *
| - | _  *  __
| - | | *      |/'
| - | |~*~~~o~|
| - | | O o *  |
/___\|o___O_ |
```

## 97. State Fair

I'm not one for roller coasters
I am not some radical dude
So if you see me at the state fair this year
It's only for the food.

```
            _.-.
          ,'/ //\
         /// // /)
        /// // //|
       /// // ///
      /// // ///
     (`: // ///
      `;`: ///
      / /:`:/
     / /   `'
    / /
   (_/
```

## 98. Tooth Fairy
The tooth fairy must be busy all the time
She deserves our kind remarks
Yes she handles our human teeth
But imagine what she does for sharks.

```
        .--.      _,
     .--;      \ /(_
    /    '.    |   '-._     . ' .
   |       \ \   ,-.)  -= * =-
   \ /\_   '. \((`  .(     '/. '
    )\ /     \ )\ _/   _/
   /  \\    .-'\__/'--. /_\
   |    \\_.'\,         /\/||
   \     \_.-';,_) _)'\ \||
    '.       /'\  (   '._/
     `\   .; |vvvv'.
      ).'  )/|        \
       `    ` | \|   |
              \  |   |
               '.|   |
                 \  '\__
                  `-._  '._ _
                    \`;-.`` ._
                     \ \ `'-._\
                      \ |
                       \ )
                        \_\
```

## 99. Ninety Nine Bottles

Ninety nine bottles of pop on the wall
I'm assuming they're on a shelf
Drink them in moderation please
Cause soda is bad for your health

Ninety nine bottles of pop on the wall
But we also have water too
It's better for your body of course
But hey, that's up to you

Ninety nine bottles of pop on the wall
Don't let them go to waste
It's fine, drink one, just brush your teeth
Make sure you use toothpaste.

```
              _
            | = |
            |   |
            |   |
           /     \
          .       .
          | ----- |
          |  POP  |
          | ----- |
          |_____|
       ===============
         | = |     | = |
         |   |     |   |
         |   |     |   |
        /     \   /     \
       .       . .       .
       | ----- | | ----- |
       |  POP  | |  POP  |
       | ----- | | ----- |
       |_____| |_____|
       =====================
```

## 100. Sticks and Stones

"Sticks and stone may break my bones
But words will never hurt me"
Though they can stick up in your mind
And that can be almost worse, see

So watch the things you say to others
You don't want the wrong thing to stick
Think of kindness and compliments
There's plenty of nice things to pick

"My, you sure have a wonderful smile"
"I love what you've done with your hair"
"Such a lovely dress, where'd you get it?"
"Have a nice day, now please take care!"

It's easy to say a thing that's wrong
But the same goes for things that are right
So be mindful of which of your words may stick
And always be kind and polite.

```
      . - .
     (o.o)
      |=|
     __|__
   //.=|=.\\
  //  .=|=.  \\
  \\  .=|=.  //
    \\(_=_)//
     (:|  |:)
      ||  ||
      ()  ()
      ||  ||
      ||  ||
     =='  '==
```

## 101. Fast Food

Fast food sounds good today
If you wanna go I'll meet ya
Be sure to bring your running shoes
I strapped a burger to a cheetah.

## 102. Diagnosed SBD

Flatulence sounds like a medical condition
Something a doctor could diagnose
Like, "My doctor just said I have flatulence
The prescription is to hold your nose."

"I contracted it." the doc said
I said, "I don't know what that means."
Then he said, "It seems my friend
You've had too many beans."

But my flatulence isn't contagious
So you're safe there's nothing to fear
I mean, just as long as you go quick
And stand off over there

It isn't life threatening either
But the doctor called it S.B.D
I got diagnosed with flatulence today
So distance yourselves from me.

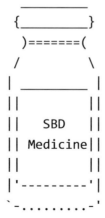

### 103. Bacon

Bacon flavored bubble gum
And bacon scented soap
There's bacon flavored toothpaste
That still cleans teeth I hope

There's bacon band aids for boo boos
And bacon chapstick for lips
Bacon soda to quench your thirst
Go on and take some sips

There's bacon flavored ice cream
There's bacon all about
I think it's bacon me crazy
Oh my, I think I'm bacon-ed out.

## 104. Groundfly

If the sky was falling well that'd be fine
Since clouds are just fog, thats why
The opposite of which would be so much worse
If the ground flew up into the sky

Skyfall will always beat groundfly
I do feel this idea is sound
For I'd rather have a nice sunset fall
Than a mountain flying around.

```
       _____
      |                      - (  |
  ,'-.                      .  `-|
 (____".           ,-.       '   ||
      |          /\,-\    ,-.    |
      |      ,-./      \ /'.-\ |
      |     /-.,\        /     \|
      |    /      \    ,-.       \
      |__/_____/_____\
```

### 105. Dark

I hope you like dark poetry
For this is much darker than most
Nightfall in dense wilderness
Far beyond burnt toast

Permanent markers black as can be
A lump of coal before a fire
A crow flying right over your head
A brand spankin' new car tire

A cute black cat meowing away
A bat in a cave upside down
A leather belt or boot perhaps
A light switch pointed down.

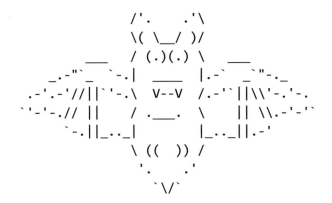

## 106. Surprise Parties Are Weird

Here's an idea
How 'bout we hide
Wait in the dark
Til someone comes inside

Leap from the corners
Jump over the couch
From sly low positions
Both laying or crouched

Scream as they enter
Decor on display
Scare them to death with a
!!!HAPPY BIRTHDAY!!!

```
            ,     ,     ,     ,
        ,  |_,_|_,_|_,_|  ,
     _,-=|;   |,   |,   |,   |;=-_
   .-_| , | , | , | , | , |   _-.
   |:  -|:._|___|___|__.|:=-   :|
   ||*:  :    .     .    :  |*||
   || |  | *  |  *  |  *  | | ||
 _.-=|:*|  |   |     |    |  |*:|=-._
 -    `._:  | * |  * |  * |  :_.'    -
 =_       -=:.___:_____|___.: =-     _=
     -  .  _  __  ___   ___   __ _ .  -
```

## 107. False Alarm

The restaurant is on fire
Smoke is in the air
No one seems frightened
Does no one else care

The fire is getting closer
Hear it crackling hot
False alarm, sorry
It's the fajitas I got.

## 108. Butterflies

I must have swallowed caterpillars
One night while I was sleeping
Cause for someone reason in my belly
I can feel them creeping

It really only happens
When I see this girl at school
The caterpillars get to crawling
Then I look like a fool

The more I am around her
They grow, I don't know how
But I think I, without a doubt
Have full blown butterflies now.

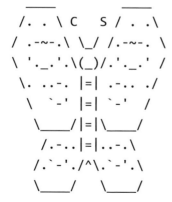

### 109. Bingo

Bingo ringo tingo tango
Ringo pingo jingo jango
Zangy zingers bling and bing
Gee, you will read anything.

## 110. Font

Express yourselves

*With words and thought*

*Have fun and choose*

A WACKY FONT

Whether **silly** or **serious**

*Just pick from the lot*

Get writing, get going

**SHOW THE WORLD WHAT YOU'VE GOT!**

```
+--------------+
|.------------.|
||  09.18.13  ||
||  08.04.16  ||
||  11.27.19  ||
||  03.02.95  ||
|+------------+|
+-.,--------..-+
  .------------.
 / /==========\ \
/ /============\ \
/_____\
_____/
```

## 111. Favors

"Can you do me a favor" is a dangerous question
Be careful before you say yes
Listen to the other person first
Before you're stuck in a mess

I don't care if it's your family
And I don't care if it's your friends
When someone asks you for a favor
Answer always, "Depends."

How strange, how odd, how different
How abnormal, how weird, some say
But nay, I reply, it's simply smart
I promise you'll thank me one day.

```
              . . . . . .
           . : | | | | | | | | : .
          /                   \
         (    o        o    )
  - -@@@@- - - - - - - - - : :- - - - - - - - -@@@@- -
```

### 112. Senses

You've heard the five basic senses
Taste, touch, sight, hearing and smell
But there are many more senses you have
Now you may be thinking, "Do tell."

Thermoception allows to you to feel
Whether things may be cold or hot
Proprioception is how you know
Where body parts are that you've got

Equilibrioception is balance and gravity
There's pressure, hunger and thirst
Nociception is pain like cavities
Which is probably the worst

They say there might be over fifty
But I saved one sense for last
Your sense of time is how you tell
how much time has passed.

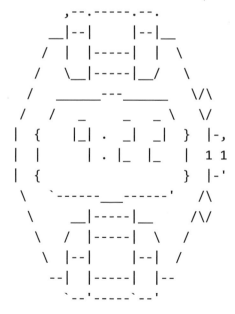

## 113. Life is a Highway

If life is a highway
Then I hope I get stuck in traffic
Cause getting where I'm going too fast
Would be tragic.

## 114. Sincerely Insincere

I hope when you drive you see only green lights
I wish when you sleep you get rest
I hope you never have to eat end slices of bread
I wish in your life all the best

I hope you find one hundred dollar bills
When you're walking down any street
I wish only compliments enter your ears
From anyone you'll ever meet

I wish the best weather over your head
No rainy days falling on you
I hope your life is filled with sun and shine
Skies filled with clouds and blue

I wish you to be happy all of the time
Without a tear of fear
Of course, I'm being serious
Sincerely, insincere.

## 115. Water

I am sixty percent water
But I don't know if I agree
Because I don't taste like water
And water doesn't taste like me

My sweat tastes kinda salty
I can't taste my own spit
But I know the taste of water
And that surely isn't it

I guess I taste like the ocean
Well, minus all the fish
Maybe I really am water
Just not the kind I wish.

```
  _\/_                    |                    _\/_
  /o\\               \         /               //o\
   |                                            |
  _|_____          .---.                 _____|__
              --  /       \  --
           `~~^~^~^~^~^~^~^~^~^~^~^~^~^~^~`
```

## 116. Megalodon

Megalodons lived twenty million years ago
Their bodies stretched out sixty feet
They were giant sharks like in sci-fi shows
Their mouths had over two hundred teeth

They were around the size of a school bus
Their teeth were the size of my palm
But don't worry they're totally extinct now
So relax, it's okay, keep calm.

They were the oceans biggest predators
Though they have come and gone
Oh, history will never soon forget
The late great Megalodon.

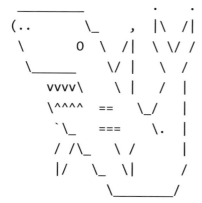

## 117. Girlscouts

Thin Mints and Tagalongs
Do-si-doe-s galore
Trefoil Shortbreads
Girl Scout outside a store

Oh, I know she's gonna ask
But no, I don't have any cash
My oh my, how to decline
That girl wearing a sash

"Smores ma'am! Somoas sir!"
Why is walking by so hard
Boy, those cookies sure look good
"Do you take Mastercard?"

```
                _   _
             _/0\/ \_
     .-.     .-` \_/\0/ '-.
    /:::\ / ,_____,  \
   /\:::/ \  '. (:::/   `'-;
   \ `-'`\ '._  `"'"'\___    \
    `'-.  \    `)-=-=(  `,    |
       \   `-"`      `"-`   /
```

### 118. Basketball

Why is basketball called basketball
Well back in eighteen ninety one
It seems that Dr. James Naismith
Who was Canadian for one

Made up an indoor sport
To enjoy when winter's cold
With peach baskets and a ball
When he was thirty one years old

He divided teams into nines
He nailed a basket to a rail
He made up rules for a brand new game
He went into detail

Then eventually there was an N.B.L
Which is now the N.B.A
All because some random guy
Made up a game one day.

```
                    _____
    o          |     __    |
      \_  0 |   |__|   |
____/ \ |___WW___|
__/   /      | |
             | |
             | |
_____| |_____
```

<u>119. I Can't Even</u>
I literally can't even
I most certainly cannot
Even if I could even
It is evens I don't got

When will I even even?
Even I don't even know
My, I just can't even now
Try to even? How 'bout no

Perhaps maybe I'll even out
Eventually this evening
O.M.G I can't even so much
Even even has lost its meaning.

```
  . . . . ,         , . . . .
 . ' , , , ' .     . ' , , , ' .
  .   `     .       .   `     .
 : . . . . . :     : . . . . . :
 :`~'-'-`:         :`-'-'~`:
  `.~-`.'           `.~`'.'
    ` ` `             ` ` `
              ____
         ( . . )


        . . _ . .
      . '       ' .
    `.~~~~~~~.`
      `-...-`
```

### 120. Exploiting a Genie

Let's say you find a lamp
Which you rub as one would do
Then suddenly a genie emerges
With three wishes for you

How would you get unlimited wishes?
Cause you know you can't wish for more
Well pay attention cause I feel
That these would work for sure

Wish every time a wish was granted
That the genie just forgot
That way after other wishes
He'll think two is what you got

Or wish for unlimited genie lamps
Then when one genie is spent
Just go grab another lamp
From a pile in the basement

How about you wish that when you wish
On a star it always came true
That way the genie isn't granting wishes
It's space that's granting you.

Not sure if this will ever help
And overthinking this might be dumb
But if you get unlimited wishes
You definitely owe me some.

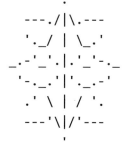

## 121. F.o.m.o.phobia

Missy misses out everything
She feels without a doubt
She's developed f.o.m.o.phobia
The fear of missing out

Missy missed the bus this morning
She missed a movie after school
Her f.o.m.o.phobia is acting wild
Did she miss seeing something cool?

Missy missed a game last weekend
She missed a party with a friend
Missy freaked out in her bedroom
Will the missing ever end?

Missy never stopped to think
During her f.o.m.o.phobic swings
All the things she missed out on
Fearing missing out on things.

```
              _
           (( ))
         (((( ))))
        ((( o.o )))
        (((\_-_/)))
        (((_) (_)))
       /((( \ / )))\
      /  (((  ^  ))) \
     / / ((  ^  ))  \ \
    ( (   \  ^  /    ) )
     \ \   )___(   / /
      `\\ /      \ //'
```

## 122. Space

Everybody needs their space
And some time to be alone
Or perhaps some space to live in
Like an apartment or a home

They need space between their words
And space for things they've got
Some people need space literally
We call them astronauts.

```
                _ · · · _
             · '           ' ·
         /        · - " " - \      _ / \
      · - |      / : ·     |    |    |
      |   \    | : ·     / · - ' - · /
      |  · - ' - ; : __ · '        = /
       · ' =    * = | NASA _ · = '
      /      _ ·    |     ;
     ; - · - ' |      \    |
     /    | \      _ \   _ \
     \ _ / ' · _ ; ·    = = '   = = \
          \        \    |
           /     /    /
          / - · _ / - · _ /
          \       ` \   \
            ` - · _ / · _ /
```

### 123. Hairy Hippopotamus

We saw a hairy hippopotamus
Wandering wooded brush
We stopped still in our tracks
And everyone went hush

It had four giant legs
With giant hippo paws
On the tips of his hippo toes
Were giant hippo claws

It had tiny hippo ears
Covered in furry hippo hair
T'was the weirdest hippo I'd seen
For it looked just like a bear.

## 124. Bright Sides

There's a bright side to everything
Just use an imaginative eye
It's easy to do, that I promise you
All you need to do is try

So let's say your on a plane
Then the engine decides to blow
Don't you freak, wow this is neat
A mid flight fire show

So then the plane starts to dive
And fall instead of climb
Well buttercup, let's buckle up
It's roller coaster time

So the plane lands in the Pacific
Then you'll go evacuate outside
No boo hoos, only good for you's
Complimentary water slide

And if that's not a silver lining
I don't believe you in the slightest
Cause if you're alive at the end of the day
That side should be your brightest.

```
        __|__
--o--o--(_)--o--o--
```

## 125. Ts and Vs

If T-shirts are T-shirts since they look like Ts
Why don't we say V-pants since they look like Vs
Shoes can be commas or dashes with lace
Of course shorts are Vs too. Just lower case.

```
,==C==.
|_/|\_|
|´|` |
|  |  |
|  |  |
|__|__|
```

<u>126. Growl</u>
My stomach angrily growled at me
So I fed him a tasty quiche
Then I took him outside the house a bit
And walked him on his leash

I gave him some water after our stroll
And let him rest up on the couch
But then he growled again at me
Boy, he sure can be a grouch.

```
      .- - - - - - - - - - - - .- - - - - - - - - - - - .
      |                  |                  |
      |      **          |      **          |
      |                  |                  |
      |_____|_____|
     /                                       \
    /                                         \
   /_____\
   |                                          |
   |_____|
  []                                          []
```

## 127. The Lawn

I moo'd the lawn today
And no that is not a typo
I took a cow by her feet
Then let her eat like there's no tomorrow.

```
        __n__n__
   .-------`-\00/-'
  /   ##   ## (oo)
 / \##  __    ./
   |//YY \|/
    |||    |||
```

### 128. The Feud

I bet the guy who invented high fives
Probably hated the fist bump dude
They most likely didn't get along too well
There was probably a feud

But no matter the amount they disliked each other
No matter their ages or growth
There was only one person who hated much more
For the handshake man hated them both.

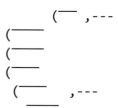

## 129. Unhinged

I opened my jaw so wide
So wide it nearly unhinged
I swear if you'd of seen it
You would have likely cringed

You would've seen my teeth
You would've seen my tongue
You would've seen my uvula
In the back where it is hung

I sucked in all the air I could
Pushed it out til it was gone
My how weird a thing it is
The thing being a yawn.

```
                                    Z
                              Z
        .,.,              Z
     ((((((())      z
     ((('_  _`) '
     ((G   \ |)
     (((`    " ,
     .((\.:~:              .-------------.
     __.| `"'.__        | \             |
   .~~    `---'  ~.     | .             :
   /              `    |  `-._____)
   |          ~        |  :             :
   |                   |  :  |
   |     _             |  |  [ ## :
   \   ~~-.            |  ,   oo_____.'
    `_  ( \) _____/~~~~ `--___
    | ~`-) ) `-.  `--- ( - _:_ -
```

<u>130. Isn't It Odd</u>
No one said I had to rhyme
No one told me to
But isn't it just a little odd
When I don't.

...

Want me to rhyme?
I won't.

...

Oh wait.

...

Dangit.

```
///-\\\
|^    ^|
|0    0|
|   ~ *SNAP*!
 \ 0 /
  | |
```

### 131. Half Off

I got some clothes half off today
But it wasn't a deal for me
My shirt got stuck around my head
So now I can barely see

My pants fell around my ankles too
So it's really hard to walk
I lost one shoe during the snafu
Now I'm in a sneaker and a sock.

### 132. Famparies
Can fairies turn into vampires
I'm asking cause I caught one outside
The fairy flew up to my leg
Then bit me on my thigh

I caught her in a jar I had
After she had fed on me awhile
I caught a Fampairy today
And my Doc said I have West Nile.

### 133. Roundabout

I drove right past my exit
So I turned around to where I began
Then I drove right past my exit
Again and again and again

I went in circle after circle
Round and round a thousand times
Passing the same twenty seven trees
Driving the same white painted lines

Oh, my eyes are beginning to water
My stomach is starting to turn
I've been turning my steering wheel so long
My hands are starting to burn

Why can I not get this right?
How can I not figure this out?
I've been trapped for over an hour now
Stuck driving this roundabout.

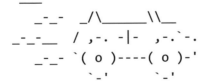

## 134. Clock In

My job told me to clock in
So I brought my grandfather clock
Old and wooden with golden trim
But all anyone did was mock

No one else brought in their clocks
Not even watches on wrists or in pockets
Not a cuckoo in sight, not one on a wall
No electrics plugged into their sockets

Now it rings hourly from my desk
And everyone can hear the song
But I can't help it, it's what it does,
"Ding dong! Ding dong! Ding Dong!"

"Clocking in is just documenting entry
And I should probably make this known
Tomorrow when you come in would you
Leave your grandfather clock at home"

I nodded at my boss's request
The grandfather clock struck it's chime
That's when my boss looked up and said
"I appreciate your time."

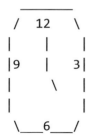

## 135. Specifics

I am the strongest man who ever lived
In the shoes that I currently wear
I am the smartest guy in the entire world
If you're only looking right here

I'm the number one star athlete
With my exact name in my town
I'm the best guitar player to ever live
Who's ever heard my sound

Out of all with my birthday and birthmark
I am the most attractive that I know
I am the richest man out of anyone
With my legs and arms and torso

I'm the headest honcho, the biggest cheese
The most astoundingly terrific
Only if and only if
I am super oddly specific.

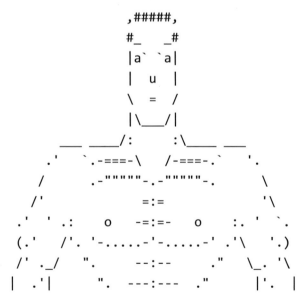

## 136. Fight Night

I didn't expect to get caught in a fight
But I found myself stuck in its wake
My Brain, Heart and Stomach collided
Over a piece of chocolate cake

'You're hungry!" Stomach yelled aloud
"It's your favorite!" Heart did burst
"No!" Brain interjected them both,
"You're bored! Perhaps it's thirst!"

"Don't listen to him" Stomach gurgled,
Heart puffed, "You'll feel better you know?"
"Stop toying with the boy" Brain did strain,
"He ate not long ago."

"What do you know?" Stomach growled at him
"Beat it!" Heart pumped his voice
"Don't do it boy" Brain calmly said
"You always have a choice."

"It's two against one" Heart boasted Brain
Stomach angrily roared, **"Feed me!"**
That's when I shut my refrigerator door
And went to watch some TV.

"That's my boy!" Brain chirped and sang
Heart pouted, "Man this is whack!"
That's when stomach whispered soft
"Don't worry Heart, he'll be back..."


```
   ,d88b.d88b,
  88888888888
  `Y8888888Y'
    `Y888Y'
      `Y'
```

### 137. Pepperoncini

Why do they put peppers in pizza boxes?
What's the purpose behind the thought?
Why is it that a spicy pepper
Tags along with the pizza I bought?

Well as it turns out back in the 90's
There was a man named John Schnatter
Who worked for a pub called Rocky Sub's
Which doesn't really matter

For Schnatter became known as Papa John
A pizza mogul at best
And a thing he did seemed quite different
Different from all the rest

He garnished every pie with a pepperoncini
Since it didn't cost too much
His customers appreciated the single pepper
As a little nice extra touch

So why are peppers in pizza boxes?
Pretty much because it was cool to do
Papa John just chose a signature
I wonder what will signify you.

### 138. An Open Ear is Everything

I've heard that talk is cheap
But I don't believe that to be
I feel that listening has value
I think that talking is just free

An open ear is everything
An open mouth is expectation
It's free to flap your gums about
But what's valuable is your attention

If you're reading this then I've got it
Joy, what a happy day for me
Who in life pays you attention?
Oh, how special they must be.


```
        . - - . _
    ( ( / - - - . _ )
    ( _ / Q  Q  )
    /  | c   /
   / - \ . - , - ' - , . __
   \ - -    o - - - o  - - \
    \ _ _ ,  H - - - H (  - - \
           \ \ - - \ - \ _ _ - \
            \ \ - - \  - / \ _ / )
             \ o - o - - \  ( ( \
```

"Honestly you can trust me
I'd never tell a lie"
Honestly just trust me
Don't ever trust that guy.

```
      _//////|\\\\\_
     ////////|\\\\\\\\
    |////////|\\\\\\\\|
    |    ___      ___    |
    |   - o -    - o -   |
    |    """      """     |
    |         \          |
    |       '---'        |
     \  ._____.   /
       .  \_____/   .
         _        _
        "-_____-"
         |      |
      __--'      '--__
```

140. Commercial Break
Advertisements have made a home
Inside my memory
For instance, why do I know B.O.G.O
Stands for buy one get one free

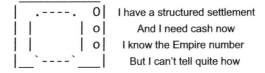

I have a structured settlement
And I need cash now
I know the Empire number
But I can't tell quite how

Sometimes I sing in the shower
The Education Connection song
Either that or I'll switch
To Free Credit Report dot com

I know where it is easy
to get a great night sleep
No credit no problem,
you can still buy a Jeep

Coocoo for Cocoa Puffs,
left and right Twix
They're after me Lucky Charms
and rabbits like Trix

Got milk? Taste the rainbow
The quicker picker upper
Snap Crackle Pop
Save money live better

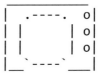

Like a good neighbor
Think outside the bun
I'm loving it, just do it
Betcha can't eat just one

I'm sure you knew at least one of these
So I've got some news for you
It seems that ads have made a home
Inside of your memory too.

<u>141. Star Signs</u>
There's Aries, Leo and Cancer
Libra, Pisces and Sagittarius
There's Virgo and then there's Gemini
Taurus and Aquarius

There's two more left to go
One star sign being Scorpio
Then there's my most favorite one
Leonardo DiCaprio.

## 142. Fishbowls

I'm glad fishbowls are called that
Just in case someone doesn't know
And accidently puts their goldfish
Where it's not supposed to go.

They could plop him in a bag
They could stuff him in a box
Without fishbowls he'd be swimming
Around in someone's dirty socks

He could end up in your cereal
Which that would be just cruel
He could wind up in the filter
If you put him in your pool

But he won't because it's obvious
Just in case you didn't know
Fishbowls are called fishbowls
Cause that's where they're supposed to go.

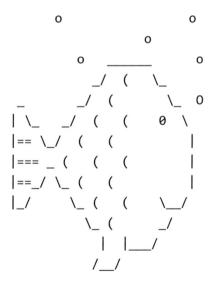

### 143. I Tried

If you're reading this then you've picked up my book
And may I say good for you
To choose this out of all the things
That you could possibly do

Of which the options are unlimited
You could be doing anything else
But for some reason here you are
Having taken my book off a shelf

Why should my thoughts have value?
Why should my words be read?
Why should people listen
To the things that I have said?

I don't mean to bum you out
Not every day can be great
Sad will turn happy eventually
If you're patient enough to wait

Now I should probably do the thing
Where I write something wacky or fun
Well I tried … But I can't today …
I'll get you on the next one.

Sorry.

## 144. Conjunctions

Conjunctions are now illegal
The law is the clearest of cuts
Don't ever use a conjunction again
No ifs ands or buts.

```
                  ,
     __   _.-"`` ` '-.
   /||\'._ __{}_(
   ||||   |'--.__\
   |  L.(    ^_\^
   \ .-' |    _ |
   | |   )\__/
   |  \-'`:._]
   \__/;        '-.
   |   |o      __ \
   |   |o     )( |
   |   |o     \/ \
```

## 145. Praise Be
Coffee coffee coffee
Morning noon and night
A boost of caffeine is all I need
To get me feeling right

Goodbye soggy foggy brain
Goodbye groggy body
Hello manic energy
Praise be to hot coffee.

```
         _.-/`)
        // / / )
     .=// / / / )
    //`/ / / / /
    // /       ` /
    ||          /
     \\        /
      ))    .'
     //    /
          /
```

### 146. Time Flies

Time flies like a soaring bird
Flowing quickly with the winds
I wish time were a flightless bird
Like chickens or maybe penguins

Perhaps time might then slow down
Even for second or two
I sure wish time were a flightless bird
Like an ostrich or an emu.

## 147. Troubleshooting

You've reached the troubleshooting page
Problem solving steps just for you
Reference this passage notated here
To resolve any experience issue

If the words placed here are upside down
Please rotate to be corrective
If you don't like a particular poem, that's fine
Everything written is subjective

If you can't see a thing please check to see
If your lights provide illumination
Also please ensure your eyelids have been
Secured in an upright position

I hope these troubleshooting steps
Get you through this book safe and sound
Speaking of which, keep your hands on the book
To prevent it from hitting the ground.

```
  |  _____   |
  |  |XXXXXXXXXXXX |   |
  |  |XXXXXXXXXXXX |   |
  |  |XXXXXXXXXXXX |   |
  |  |XXXXXXXXXXXX |   |
  |  |XXXXXXXXXXXX |   |
  |_____|
      _[_____]_
   ___[_____]___
  |          [_____] []|__
  |          [_____] []|  \__
  L_____J     \
  _____       /\
 /##################\    (__)
```

## 148. Crust

If you choose to eat pizza crust
We have no rivalry or scandal
I for one, just happen to believe
That crust is the pizza's handle.

## 149. Hit or Miss

Not every poem written is great
It's a game of hit or miss
Sometimes you write something incredible
Sometimes you write stuff like this

It's not all about what is written
Even if it's the simplest scrawl
What matter most at the end of the day
Is that you wrote anything at all.

```
                     _ _ _ _ _ _ _ _ _ _ _
        ( - ( - ( - ( - ( - ( - ( - ( - ( - ( - ( - ( )
         / ̄ - - - - - - - - -  ̄ / | |
        /                        / _ | |
       /                        / _ _ | |
      / / |   /                / _ _ _ | |
     / /  | /  _ _ / _ _  _    / _ _ _ | |
     / /   | / ( _ )  ( _ ( / _ / _ ) _ / _ _ _ _ | |
    / ( _ _ _ _ _ _ _ _ _ _ / _ _ _ _ | |
   /    ̄ - - - - - - - - -  ̄ / _ _ _ _ _ | |
  /                          / _ _ _ _ _ _ | |
 /                          / _ _ _ _ _ _ _ | |
 ( _ _ _ _ _ _ _ _ _ _ _ _ _ ( _ _ _ _ _ _ _ | |
           | _ _ _ _ _ _ _ _ _ _ _ _ _ _ | |
           | _ _ _ _ _ _ _ _ _ _ _ _ _ _ | |
           | _ _ _ _ _ _ _ _ _ _ _ _ _ _ | |
           | _ _ _ _ _ _ _ _ _ _ _ _ _ _ | |
           | _ _ _ _ _ _ _ _ _ _ _ _ _ _ | |
           | _ _ _ _ _ _ _ _ _ _ _ _ _ _ | /
```

## 150. WWYD

What would you do for a Klondike Bar
Is a question I do not take lightly
At an almost philosophical level
I ponder the conundrum nightly

I eventually came to a conclusion
Which is not meant to be funny
You don't have to do anything for a Klondike Bar
That you couldn't just do for money.

```
                __ _____ __
       ..;;;--'~~~`--;;;..
      /;-~IN GOD WE TRUST~-.\
    //       ,;;;;;;;;;       \\
  .//       ;;;;;     \        \\
  ||       ;;;;;(   /.|         ||
  ||       ;;;;;;;   _\         ||
  ||       ';;  ;;;;;=          ||
  ||LIBERTY |  ''\;;;;;;;       ||
   \\     ,| '\  '|><| 2013 //
    \\   |    |      \  A //
     `;.,|.    |      '\.-'/
      ~~;;;,._|___.,-;;;~'
          ''=--'
```

### 151. Selfie

I scrolled through all my photos
I saw selfie after selfie
And thought the person inside them
Almost looked exactly like me

Something about them was different though
As I scrolled for well over a mile
Something just didn't feel quite right
About the way they seemed to smile

I know I wasn't happy there
I know I wasn't happy then
But there I was in a selfie pic
With that forced and toothy grin

I came to see the photos weren't me
They were a version of myself without
Everything that had ever made me *me*
Every fear and tear and doubt

So if you're scrolling through and you see me
Trapped inside a selfie
Just know I guess that's a pic of me
But then again… not exactly.

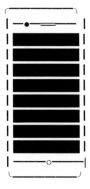

### 152. Avocado Toast

Provide as little as possible
Get consumers to pay the most
I feel that is the business strategy
With avocado toast

And I know you never needed to know this
And sharing this fact won't change a thing
But Americans spent 900,000 a month
On avocado toast in 2017

Now you know and who knows why
What can you do with this information?
I guess maybe you could randomly
Bring it up in conversation.

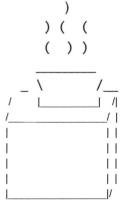

### 153. Would You Rather?

Would you rather have a big dog in your house
Snarling and rabid with rabies
Or would you rather have a venomous spider crawl in
And have a thousand babies?

Would you rather eat a cheesecake
Made entirely of cheddar cheese?
Or would you rather eat a handful
Of chocolate covered peas?

Would you rather skydive in a chicken suit
To prove that chickens can fly?
Or would you rather ride every roller coaster
Sitting next to an orthodox rabbi?

Would you rather sneeze when you hear please
Or would you rather fart viewing art?
Would you rather play Would You Rather all day
Or would you rather not even start?

## 154. Flower

From a splitting crack in the sidewalk
I saw a flower growing through
And if a flower could bust through cement like that
I sure wonder what I could do

Cause if something so soft and simple
Can get through something so hard and rough
Then I think maybe someone like me
Can get through the times that are tough.

## 155. The Worst Thing

What's the worst thing that could happen?
I mean what is the absolute worst thing?
Is it moving to another town?
Is it losing a cherished ring?

Is it your car breaking down on you?
Is it dropping your brand new phone?
Is it a hole in your favorite sweater?
Is it crashing a fancy drone?

Is it missing that raging party?
Is it losing the biggest game?
Is it being broken up with?
Is it being called a name?

Is it burning food in the oven?
Is it getting sick or hurt?
Is it running out of money?
Is it being fired from your work?

I know the worst thing that could happen for me
And when it happened there was nothing I could do
But sit and experience the absolute worst thing
Of saying goodbye to you.

```
    ,-=-.          _____      _
   /  +  \     />----->  _|C|_
   |I.L.Y|    // -/- /   |_ A _|
   |R.I.P|    // / /      |S|
 \vV,,|_____|V,//____/VvV,v,|_|/,,
```

### 156. Palate Cleanser (Observational Comedy)
Woah that last poem got deep
Perhaps it's time for a palate cleanser
Have you noticed that public restrooms
Have inefficient towel dispensers?

Nothing like observational comedy
To help realign the sights
But seriously, those towel dispensers
Ha! Come on now. Am I right?

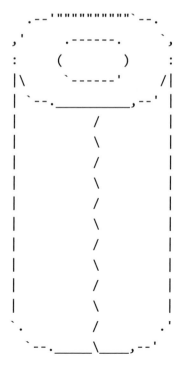

## 157. Puppets

People are like puppets
They can be pulled with string
Some can be manipulated
Though it's a terrible, horrible thing

Unlike puppets, you can't make us talk
And this is the case, no matter what
Only because there is a lot of space
Between our mouths and our butts.

### 158. Dinner

Do you want to make a soup?
Do you want to make a stew?
What do you want for dinner tonight?
I don't know, well how 'bout you?

What if we pop in a pizza?
Maybe we can throw in a pie?
Perhaps a sandwich would be nice
On some pumpernickel or rye

Perhaps a layered lasagna
Or a steamy pasta dish
Maybe a salad with bacon bits
Or anything you wish

If there are too many things to choose from
It's nothing to stress over right?
I say we don't cook a single thing
We'll just have leftovers tonight.

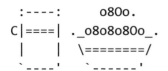

```
 :----:      o8Oo.
C|====| ._o8o8o8Oo_.
 |    | \========/
 `----'   `------'
```

## 159. One Word

A food made of batter or dough
Cooked between two patterned plates
Served usually with syrup and butter
To add more flavor to taste

A failure to make up one's mind
Which can be just embarrassingly awful
What do these two things have in common?
One word...

Waffle.

```
         _.-------._
      .'  | | | |  '.
     / _| | | | | |_ \
    | | | | | | | | | |
    |_| | | | | | | |_| |
    | |_| | | | | | | | |
    | |_| | | | | | |_| |
     \ -| | | | | |- /
      '. -| | | |- .'
        `._____.`
```

## 160. The Last One
I know what comes after this
But I don't know if I am ready
I knew we would get here eventually
I knew where this was heading

So I appreciate you reading this
Thank you for stopping by
I hope you can take something away from this
Now that it's time we say goodbye

Perhaps you'll try to hide in the garbage bin
Maybe go chase your chair
I hope you take whisks from here on out
And know I'm okay back here

Remember that time isn't everything
And a can can can a man
Remember not to invest in storks
And pirate Cap'n Dan

I'm glad you're out in the future somewhere
I hope it's everything and more
But I think it's time we say goodbye
So do me a favor and shut the door.

```
>>>>>>>_____\`-._
>>>>>>>       (Turn the page.)   /.-'
```

THE

END

Printed in Great Britain
by Amazon